SURFING MOODS
Catching the Best Waves in the Westcountry

Jon Bowen

HALSGROVE

First published in Great Britain in 2006

British Library Cataloguing-in-Publication Data
A CIP record for this title is available from the British Library

ISBN 1 84114 558 0
ISBN 978 1 84114 558 7

HALSGROVE
Halsgrove House
Lower Moor Way
Tiverton, Devon EX16 6SS
Tel: 01884 243242
Fax: 01884 243325
email: sales@halsgrove.com
website: www.halsgrove.com

Printed and bound by D'Auria Industrie Grafiche Spa, Italy

Introduction

The south west peninsula of England has an embarrassment of riches in beaches and surf. We have long golden beaches and rugged cliffs, hidden coves and offshore reefs. As the sport of surfing becomes more popular, the famous surfing beaches of Newquay or Croyde become more cramped, but for those willing to explore there are empty waves to be had.

Waves are elemental things that touch something primeval within human beings. The sheer raw power on display when open ocean waves exhaust themselves on the beach draws people towards them. Dangerous, yet fascinating. It's this visceral energy that surfers experience more directly than anyone, riding these ripples of energy at their last gasp across the sea. In this book I have tried to capture some of the exhilaration and the adrenaline-charged moments of concentration of a barreled shortboarder, or the carving grace of a longboarder. I also hope to try to share the surfer's fascination with the endless variation and permutations of shape that breaking waves form.

I have surfed for most of my life, and it has taken me to places I never thought I'd visit and led me to discover beauty so close to home that I'd never otherwise have reason to find. I've met fascinating, adventurous and crazy people, some so surf-obsessed they are willing to make all sorts of sacrifices just to be able to ride waves on a daily basis. Others, more commonly, strive to balance the obligations of life – work, relationships, food, sleep – with the insatiable appetite to ride waves. When the sun goes down in the evening, every surfer in the water longs for just one more hour of light, just one more wave.

I have also taken photographs for as long as I can remember, and it was a natural progression that the two should coincide. To go surfing, all you need is a board, wetsuit, and waves. However to take photographs you need an awkward load of expensive and reasonably delicate equipment. Salt water is the ultimate solvent. Given enough time the sea can dissolve a battleship and it can destroy a £1000 lens in considerably less time! Surfing is a relatively cheap sport. Photography most certainly isn't, and surf photography is very hard on equipment. Salt, wind and sand, not to mention getting just a 'bit' too close to the action, can have expensive consequences. Photographers who surf also have a dilemma: if the waves are good, then I want to go surfing, but I also want to take pictures of them!

Acknowledgements

Thanks to the surfers of Devon and Cornwall for being such willing subjects.
Also to Stuart Butler at Oceansurf and Rosanna Rothery at the
North Devon Journal for their encouragement and inspiration.

Secret spots are hard to find these days.
Every inch of coast has been scoured in every type
of weather and at all states of the tide, but they do
still exist. The rewards for trekking over muddy
fields, scrambling down dangerous cliffs in a howling
gale, or just summoning the motivation to actually not
follow the crowd to Croyde for a change are more
often then not a disappointment. But sometimes
it all comes together. Sunny day, empty waves,
and all to yourself.

Is it cold? If your average surfer had a pound each time this innocent question was asked we'd all have houses in Hossegor. The answer? Of course it's cold.

It's January. At this time of year the sea temperature is about 10C (40F) and an unprotected person will experience the onset of hypothermia within 10 minutes. Survival time is about an hour. So how do surfers spend hours at a time having fun in the water in the depths of winter when in theory they should be fighting for life? The answer, obviously, is a wetsuit. The modern wetsuit is an incredible piece of tailoring. Made from 'super-stretch' neoprene with elaborate and ingenious methods of doing them up to minimise the ingress of water you can comfortably spend two or three hours in the water. These days it's fatigue that drives you back to the beach rather than no longer being able to feel your feet. Of course, you still freeze solid when it comes to getting changed and you take your magical suit off in that easterly wind.

As high-performance boards become lighter, faster and more difficult to ride well, more and more surfers are rediscovering the classic longboard and leaving the hotdog aerial antics of the 90's for a more soulful surf.   Longboards are all about style and grace, long sweeping turns and board walking.

The evening session. The last half an hour of work creeps by. Surreptitious checking of the webcams on any convenient PC. Finish work right on time. Board already on the car, wetsuit still festering damp in the boot from the last session. Drive as quickly as possible. Get stuck in traffic. Curse traffic. Sun going down. A glance at the sky and the wind is picking up. Get to the beach, the first one, no time to check around. Sun on the horizon. Pull on your stinking wettie. Pull board off the roof rack. Realise the fins aren't attached. Can't find FCS key. Swear. Find key. Attach fins. Board needs waxing, ah it'll be ok. Low tide, the sea is miles away. Run. Start panting and walk for a bit. Gonna miss it! Run. Catch breath and put leash on. Paddle out — get three waves before it's too dark to see. Go home happy.

Surfing is ultimately a solitary sport. You can pile on down to the beach with all your friends, but once you've run across the sand and paddled out you enter your own space.

All those black-suited figures you see sitting on their boards out past the line of breaking waves are almost always sitting and waiting in silence, each individual almost lost in a trance. To know how to position yourself in the line-up to be in exactly the right spot to catch a wave takes patience, concentration and experience. Are you drifting out of position on the tide? Is that shadow on the horizon a set coming in? Or is it just a shadow? Do I need to move? In or out or left or right? Surfing can be a meditation — ask someone why there have chosen to wait for a wave in that specific spot, and most of the time they will find it hard to tell you. You just know, somehow, that you're in the right spot. Or you just know, somehow, you need to move 10 metres further out. You just know, unconsciously analysing the variables of wind, swell and tide, where to be.

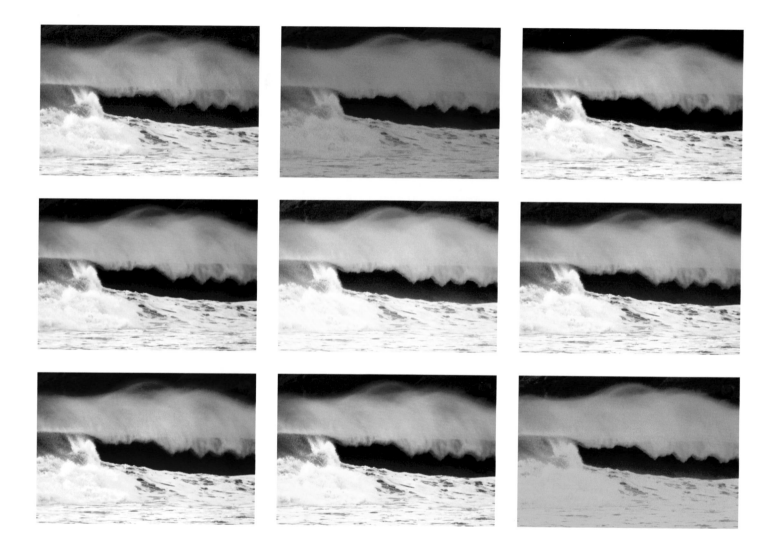

An ocean swell is pure energy. In deeper water the sea doesn't move when a swell passes through it, it just rises and falls in place as the pulse passes through like a bedsheet being flipped into place. A physicist will tell you that energy cannot be created or destroyed, it can only change form. The energy being translated across the ocean in the form of waves comes directly from the sun. The sun's heat energy warms the air, creating the winds which blow across the thousands of miles of water to form waves and so the power of the sun is transformed into those endlessly fascinating forms of water relentlessly moving across the sea. As the swells reach shore, they decelerate, crowd together, steepen and then break and the energy is transformed again into the roar of a breaking wave and the movement of sand and shingle on the beach. And a tiny percentage of that energy is tapped into by surfers, riding the last moments of a groundswell's journey.

A photograph seals a moment. Freezes it, and in the case of waves allows you to see details that are normally invisible. Droplets of water falling from a crashing lip, ripples in a face, or the fan of spray detaching from the rail of a board. But the one thing a wave, or a surfer riding that wave, can never be is motionless. Surfers manipulate the power of the moving wave, turning and trimming the board to try to extract every joule of energy so they can go as fast as possible and then release that power back into the sea with hard turns, snaps and slashes. The faster you go, the more energy you have, and the bigger the manoeuvre's possible. Speed, fluidity and motion are everything and it is what gives surfing the grace for which the sport is known and which a photograph can never fully capture.

Late take-offs are always fun. The water drops away beneath you as you slot your board in place and you feel that delicious moment of weightlessness as you drop in. Spray blinds you as you feel for the shoulder, hand-dragging the rail into the face, the g-force of your bottom turn forcing your head down. Make the drop, and you'll come out grinning. Make a mistake, and you'll be bouncing off the bottom.

How surfers measure wave height is a subject for endless discussion. Waves are measured in feet, but a surfer's idea of a foot with regards to wave height bears little resemblance to 12 inches and often tells you more about where the surfer is from rather than how big the surf is. Factor in the macho exageration which can make big surf small or tiny surf huge, depending on who's doing the telling, and it's amazing anyone ever knows what's really going on at the beach. The story is that the distortion of reported wave height came from surfers reporting that the surf was small in order to encourage people to go to a different spot, thus keeping crowds down. For most people, it boils down to three distinct sizes. Too small to surf, just right, or scary huge. It all boils down to this though: if it's big enough for you to have fun in, then really who cares?

There is something magical about the dawn patrol. Hauling yourself out of bed on an freezing cold morning to make sure you get to the beach by first light seems, at first glance, to be a completely idiotic thing to do. It is an idiotic thing to do. Why would anyone trade a warm bed for icy cold seawater? Well, because being out back sitting on your board on a crisp glassy morning, looking out to sea for the first set of the day with the sun creeping up over the hills behind you, is a magical thing. Get there insanely early, and you may have pristine surf all to yourself before anyone else makes it. Of course the planets must align and the stars explode for this to actually happen — most of the time you will have blearily staggered down the the shore at first light only to be greeted with onshore slop and driving rain — but it does happen.

Unlike most sports, you can't just throw yourself in the deep end with surfing. Before you can even think about catching a solid green wave, you have to paddle out. How to paddle, and as importantly how to duckdive, are the first skills you must learn before you can even consider catching waves. You learn how to see rips, when to paddle hard to beat a set and when to hang back to let it dissipate it's power. Getting past the barrier of tons of water falling from a great height is often difficult even for experienced surfers, and getting 'caught inside', held in the impact zone getting endlessly hammered by big waves, is a frustration shared by everyone on occasion no matter what your skill level. There are no chair-lifts in the ocean and almost making it out to the line-up, only to be blown back to the beach by the last wave in the set is hilarious when it's your mate, utterly exasperating when it's you.

Winter sucks. For surfers, it's a classic Catch 22 — The cold water thins out the crowds — but it gets dark so early that you can't make an after-work session, so everyone piles in at the weekend. Winter means deep Atlantic lows, firing in genuine swell with an open-ocean punch. But the low before that one is now sitting on top of us, throwing wind around the beach, blowing all that delicous swell out into a white-water mess. And if there is a high pressure over us? Then it's bright and crisp, without a breath of wind — and brain-seizingly cold.

Surfing requires being in the right place at the right time. You have to be at the right beach at the right time, the tide has to be right, and the swell and wind need to be right for there to be any waves in the first place. Taking it up a level, for the wind to be right the position, the sun needs to be just right to heat the air and create those winds and even the moon needs to be just right as it creates the tide.

Once the planets have aligned and you've found the right waves, you need the right board for the conditions and even once you've paddled out, you have to sit in the right place to catch the best waves — an unlikely list of coincidences if you want to get that ride. Which is why, even on the most crowded of days, a perfect unridden wave can sneak past everyone without anyone getting remotely close to catching it.

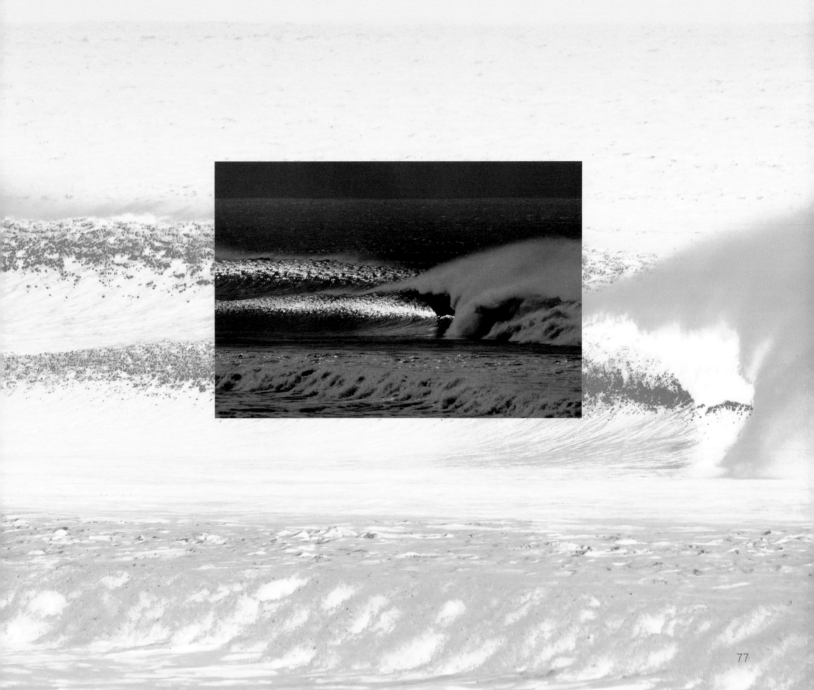

As with any sport, the younger you start the better you'll be at it. Most of the top surfing professionals were surfing as soon as they could stand, but it's not down to pushy parents. Kids love the water and when you're only 3 feet tall those unridable summer ankle-slapper waves suddenly become waist high and serious fun. Surfing has often been described as being addictive, and it's certainly no less so for the under-10 ripper. The problem isn't usally getting them into the water — it's getting them out again.

Everyone falls off. From the beginner splashing around in their first session to Kelly Slater working out how to bust a new move, everybody who surfs will find themselves whirling about under water at some point trying to work out which way is up. It can be fun, like flying weightless through watery space, being pleasantly squeezed by the water pressure. Or it can be very frightening, like going over the falls backwards on a sharp and shallow reef. But if you surf then you are going to fall off. In fact, you probably spend more time falling off than doing anything else. If you never fall, well, you're probably just not trying hard enough.

Everyone knows when a swell is coming. A global network of weather buoys, satellites, web-cams and super-computers all hooked into the internet means that even the most meteorologically illiterate surfer can instantly know what the waves are like on almost every beach on the planet. What's Pipeline like today? Maybe Kirra? One click, and you'll know. However, occasionally a swell sneaks in under the radar. There could be no storm systems within a global hemisphere from your local beach, there could be nothing out there that could be possibly producing waves. Even that weird old leather-skinned longboarder who always knows if there's swell will say it's flat. And yet, a 6 foot super-clean swell is pushing in from nowhere and the only way you'll know about it is if you're there when it arrives. Phantom swell. Impossible and empty, and a pure gift. No one knows how it got there, or where it came from.

But if you're on it, who cares?

Tube, barrel, gutter, green room, pit — surfers have dozens of names for the most sought-after experience in wave riding. To get inside the hollow, furling part of a wave and to be surrounded by moving water, and yet still be dry and be able to breathe is a profound experience. For the average surfer it's also a depressingly rare one. To ride a board into a barreling wave takes skill and timing, and to be able to generate the speed in such a confined space to ride out again takes even more skill and no small amount of luck. Surfers crave tubes and to enter one and to rush towards a droplet-shaped exit built from falling water is an experience only wave riders can know. It is also an experience so unforgettable it can condemn you to spending years trying to repeat it.

In winter you always think of those summer days. You mentally filter out the weak waves and endless flat spells from your memory and only think of those days when the lines were stacked up to the sky and you stayed out until your skin blistered and your arms turned into noodles. You also forget those summer days where you perversely wish it was winter just for the power and size of a thumping January swell, carefully forgetting the shudder of pulling on a cold, damp wetsuit in a dull grey drizzle.

The South West has a fantastic coast. Beautiful and varied, it offers everything from long lazy beachbreaks to rocky shorebreaks, to offshore reefs. If you surf you've probably seen a lot of it and probably you've seen most of it several times a day. When you go for a surf, you can never say with one hundred per cent confidence which break you'll actually end up at. You could check the weather forecast and decide that sneaky little secret spot might be working but, when you get down there, the wind isn't going quite the right way. But it's ok, you know another place that should have a slightly better wave. So you pile back in the car and head off to your number two spot, where of course, it's not quite right there either. One more place to check perhaps? Off you go again, stopping only to fuel up on Mars bars and chocolate milk. But once you get to spot three the wind has veered and now you reckon the first place you visited has probably picked up with the tide. So you turn around and, several hours later and to the incomprehensible annoyance of any non-surfers in the car, go surfing at the first beach you went to.

It's often said that Eskimos have hundreds of words to describe snow. Surfers are the same when it comes to waves. There are hundreds of words to describe a breaking wave, from official oceanographic definitions to obscure slang. An onshore wave could be sloppy, fat, slow or weak, while an offshore day could be hollow, steep, fast or heavy. Oily glass-offs are a good thing, mushy slop is not, but a report describing 'spitting kegs' would have the local wave-riding population phoning in sick and sprinting to the beach. No two waves are ever perfectly identical and the variations that wind, tide, the shape of the sea bed, swell direction, and even air and sea temperature can introduce, can together create an infinite number of wave shapes. But all these arcane descriptions are almost always answered by the one single most important question every surfer always wants to know: 'Is it ridable?

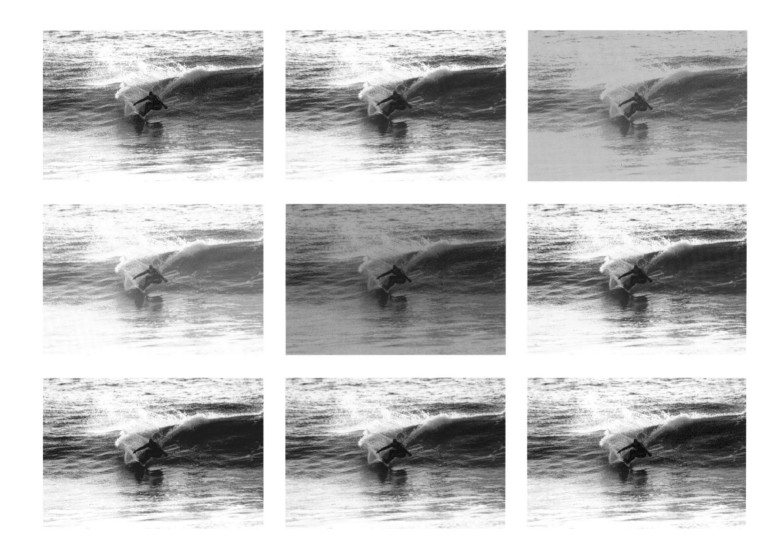

An overused to the point of cliché concept in surfing is the idea of the 'soul surfer'. Everyone likes to think they are one. Nobody actually is one. A soul surfer is a surfer who considers the act of wave-riding to be akin to a religion, or has tried to resist the commercialisation of surfing as a sport. It's the surfer with a sensible haircut who seldom says the word 'dude', yet is the best rider in the line-up. It's the guy who turns his back on society and lives on the dole, just so he can go surfing every day. It's the guy who doesn't turn up to his best friend's wedding because the waves were good that day.
A soul surfer could be all of these things, or none of them. No one is a soul surfer but everybody who surfs is a soul surfer, all at the same time.

You cannot plan to go surfing, you must wait for the waves to come. You can book time off work, take a weekend trip down the coast, but if the ocean is not so inclined you won't be going surfing. Perhaps it is this essential unpredicability, this enforced waiting, that give surfers their 'chilled out' persona. If no matter how hard you try, how much you pray, or how much effort you put in there is no guarantee you will get what you're looking for, then perhaps with that comes a level of acceptance that affects all aspects of your life. If you wait long enough, one day, the thing you are seeking will come to you, and one day, if you can wait long enough, that beach will have waves.